D0618919

TRANSLATED BY LUCIEN STRYK

PENGUIN BOOKS

PENGUIN BOOKS

Published by the Penguin Group
Penguin Books Ltd, 27 Wrights Lane, London w8 5tz, England
Penguin Books USA Inc., 375 Hudson Street, New York, New York 10014, USA
Penguin Books Australia Ltd, Ringwood, Victoria, Australia
Penguin Books Canada Ltd, 10 Alcorn Avenue, Toronto, Ontario, Canada m4v 3b2
Penguin Books (NZ) Ltd, 182–190 Wairau Road, Auckland 10, New Zealand

Penguin Books Ltd, Registered Offices: Harmondsworth, Middlesex, England

These translations of Bashō's haiku appear in
On Love and Barley: Haiku of Bashō, translated and introduced
by Lucien Stryk, published in Penguin Classics 1985
This edition published 1995
1 3 5 7 9 10 8 6 4 2

Printed in England by Clays Ltd, St Ives plc

In my new robe
this morning—
someone else.

Fields, mountains
of Hubaku, in
nine days—spring.

New Year—the Bashō-Tosei
hermitage
a-buzz with haiku.

Spring rain—
under trees
a crystal stream.

Now cat's done
mewing, bedroom's
touched by moonlight.

Do not forget the plum,
blooming
in the thicket.

Another haiku?
Yet more cherry blossoms—
not my face.

Pretending to drink
sake from my fan,
sprinkled with cherry petals.

If I'd the knack
I'd sing like
cherry flakes falling.

Under the cherry—
blossom soup,
blossom salad.

Yellow rose petals
thunder—
a waterfall.

Drizzly June—
long hair, face
sickly white.

Faceless—bones
scattered in the field,
wind cuts my flesh.

Winter downpour—
even the monkey
needs a raincoat.

First winter rain—
I plod on,
Traveller, my name.

Poet grieving over shivering
monkeys, what of this child
cast out in autumn wind?

Poor boy—leaves
moon-viewing
for rice-grinding.

Wake, butterfly—
it's late, we've miles
to go together.

Violets—
how precious on
a mountain path.

Early autumn—
rice field, ocean,
one green.

Bright moon: I
stroll around the pond—
hey, dawn has come.

Clouds—
a chance to dodge
moon-viewing.

Moon-daubed bush-clover—
ssh, in the next room
snoring prostitutes.

Bird of time—
in Kyoto, pining
for Kyoto.

Spring—through
morning mist,
what mountain's there?

Noon doze,
wall cool against
my feet.

'Now darkness falls,'
quail chirps,
'what use hawk-eyes?'

Atop the mushroom—
who knows from where—
a leaf!

Cormorant fishing:
how stirring,
how saddening.

Snowy morning—
one crow
after another.

Come, see real
flowers
of this painful world.

Summer moon—
clapping hands,
I herald dawn.

Rainy days—
silkworms droop
on mulberries.

Girl cat, so
thin on love
and barley.

Old pond,
leap-splash—
a frog.

Awaiting snow,
poets in their cups
see lightning flash.

Buddha's death-day—
old hands
clicking rosaries.

Year's end, all
corners of this
floating world, swept.

Autumn—even
birds and clouds
look old.

Loneliness—
caged cricket dangling
from the wall.

Insect song—over
winter's garden
moon's hair-thin.

Spider, are you
crying—or
the autumn wind?

Pommelling hail—
like the old oak,
I never change.

Mirroring each other:
white narcissi,
paper screen.

Such fragrance—
from where,
which tree?

How I long to see
among dawn flowers,
the face of God.

While moon sets
atop the trees,
leaves cling to rain.

Coldest days—
dried salmon,
gaunt pilgrim.

Samurai talk—
tang
of horse-radish.

You the butterfly—
I, Chuang Tzu's
dreaming heart.

Friends part
forever—wild geese
lost in cloud.

How pleasant—
just once *not* to see
Fuji through mist.

Dying cricket—
how full of
life, his song.

What stroke of luck—
hawk spied above
Irago promontory.

South Valley—
wind brings
a scent of snow.

From the heart
of the sweet peony,
a drunken bee.

Dew-drops—
how better wash away
world's dust?

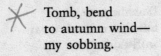

Tomb, bend
to autumn wind—
my sobbing.

Summer grasses,
all that remains
of soldiers' dreams.

Sick on a journey—
over parched fields
dreams wander on.